(my name)

loves to ______________________________

______________________________ .

This is a drawing of what I love to do.

My progress chart

As you complete each page, find the letter here. Trace the letter and draw a picture.

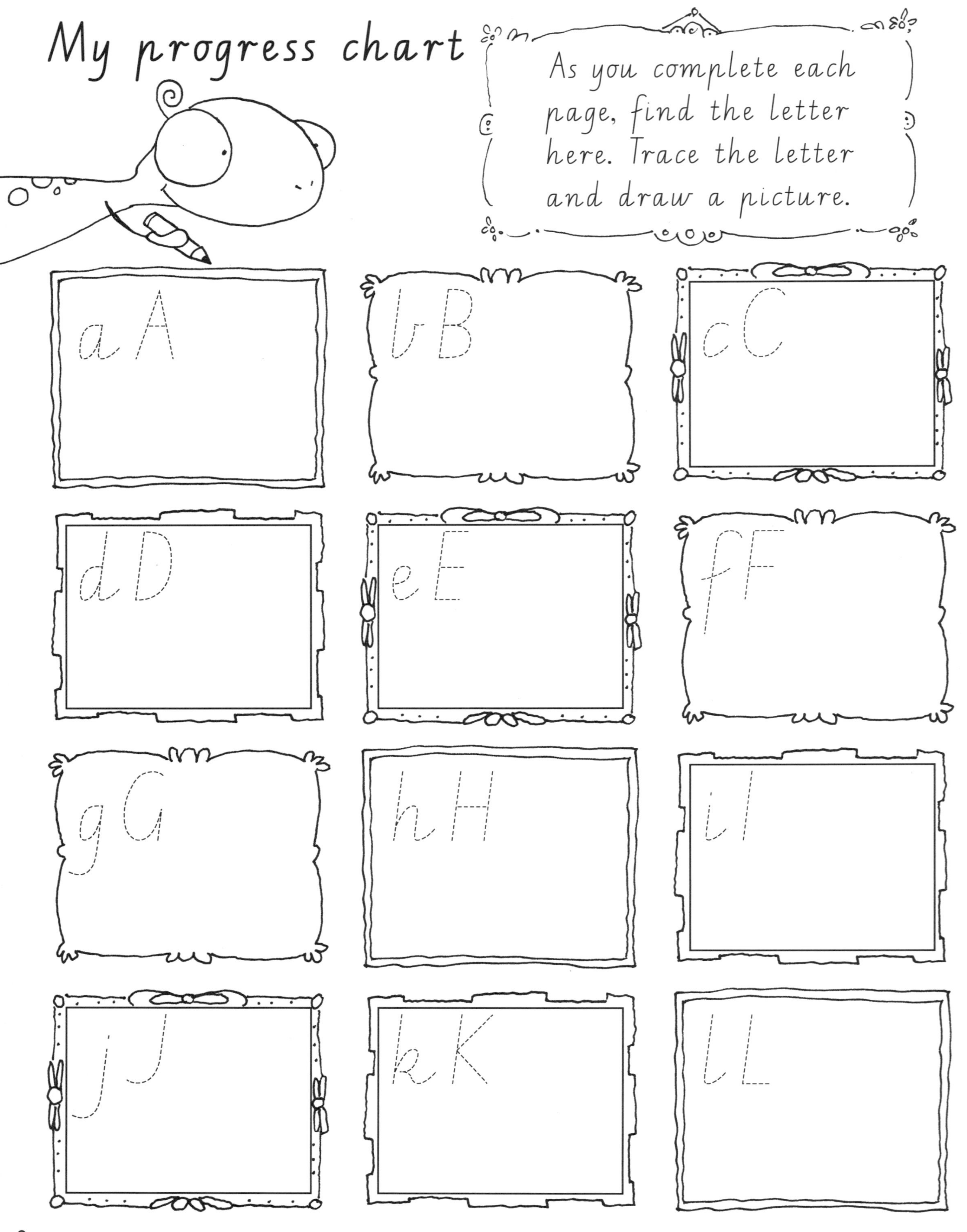

mM
nN
oO
pP
qQ
rR
sS
tT
uU
vV
wW
xX
yY
zZ

Continue the patterns. Keep your pencil on the page.

Copy the picture.

Handwriting: anticlockwise patterns.

Continue the patterns. Keep your pencil on the page.

Copy the patterns.

Handwriting: clockwise patterns.

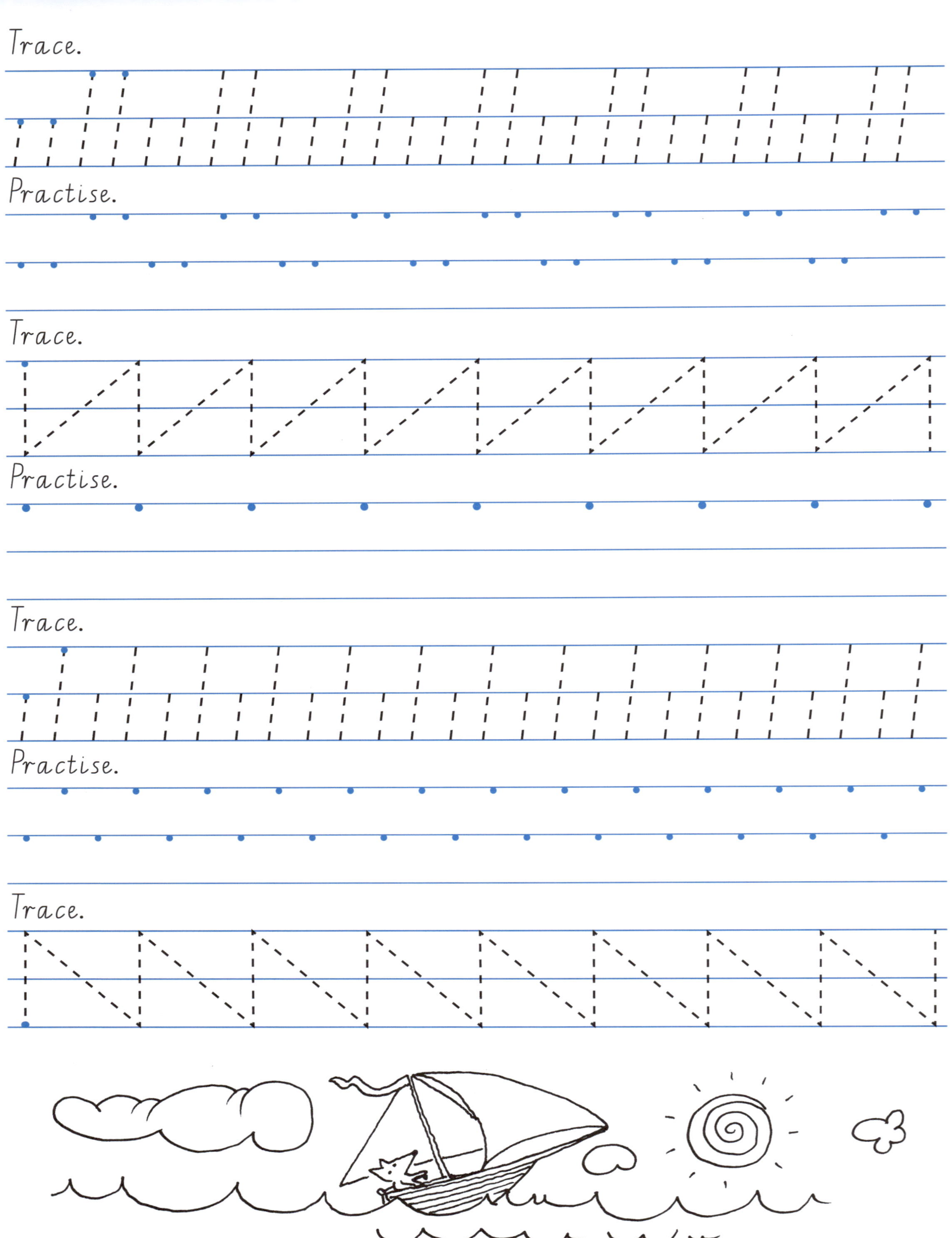

Handwriting: downstroke patterns.

Copy the patterns. Start at the dots.

Handwriting: anticlockwise letter, body letter (a).
Grammar: simple sentence, action verb (ate).
Punctuation: capital letter to start a sentence, full stop.
Spelling and vocabulary: act, again, ago, all, allow, animal, any, ape, apple, April, arm, arrow, ash, ask, ate, August.
Literary elements: alliteration.

Trace then write.

A A A

a

A

Trace then write.

An anaconda ate

all the apples.

Rate your writing.

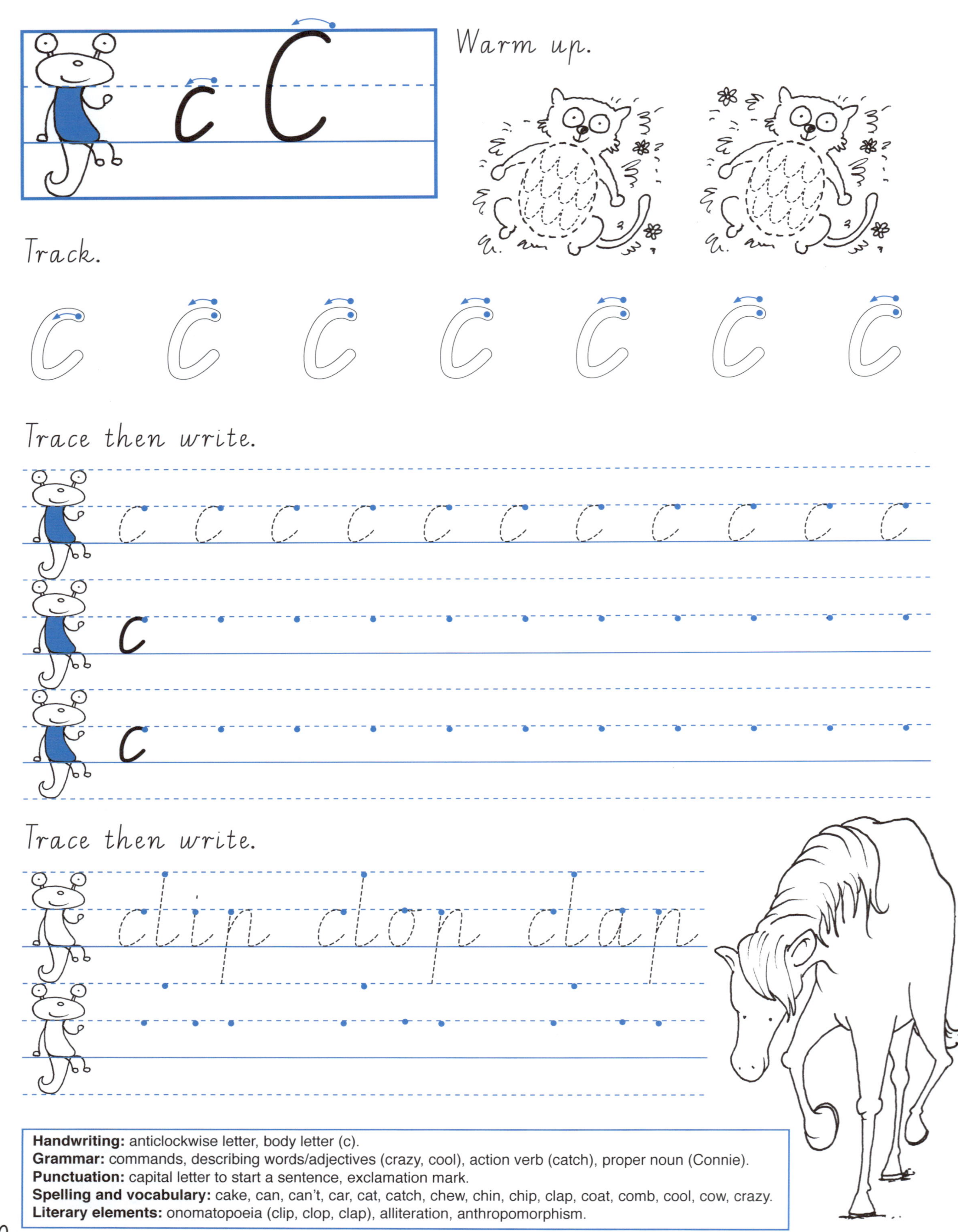

Handwriting: anticlockwise letter, body letter (c).
Grammar: commands, describing words/adjectives (crazy, cool), action verb (catch), proper noun (Connie).
Punctuation: capital letter to start a sentence, exclamation mark.
Spelling and vocabulary: cake, can, can't, car, cat, catch, chew, chin, chip, clap, coat, comb, cool, cow, crazy.
Literary elements: onomatopoeia (clip, clop, clap), alliteration, anthropomorphism.

Trace then write.

C C C

c

C

Trace then write.

Catch that crazy,

cool cow, Connie!

Rate your writing.

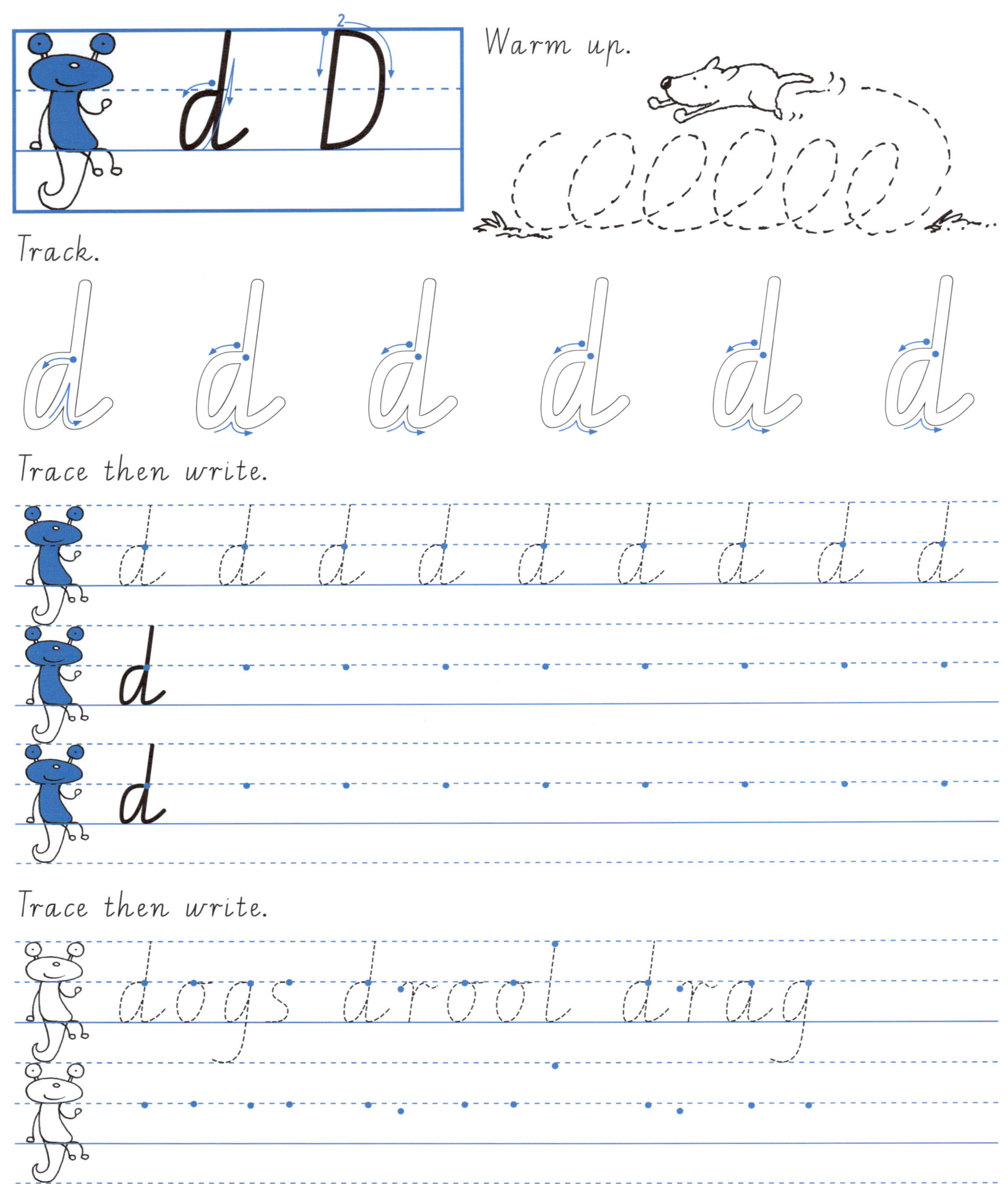

Handwriting: anticlockwise letter, head and body letter (d).
Grammar: simple sentence, statement, proper noun (Daisy), describing word/adjective (daring).
Punctuation: capital letter to start a sentence, full stop.
Spelling and vocabulary: dance, December, did, disco, do, dog, done, door, drab, drag, drip, drool, drop, drum, doll, duck.
Literary elements: alliteration, anthropomorphism.

Trace then write.

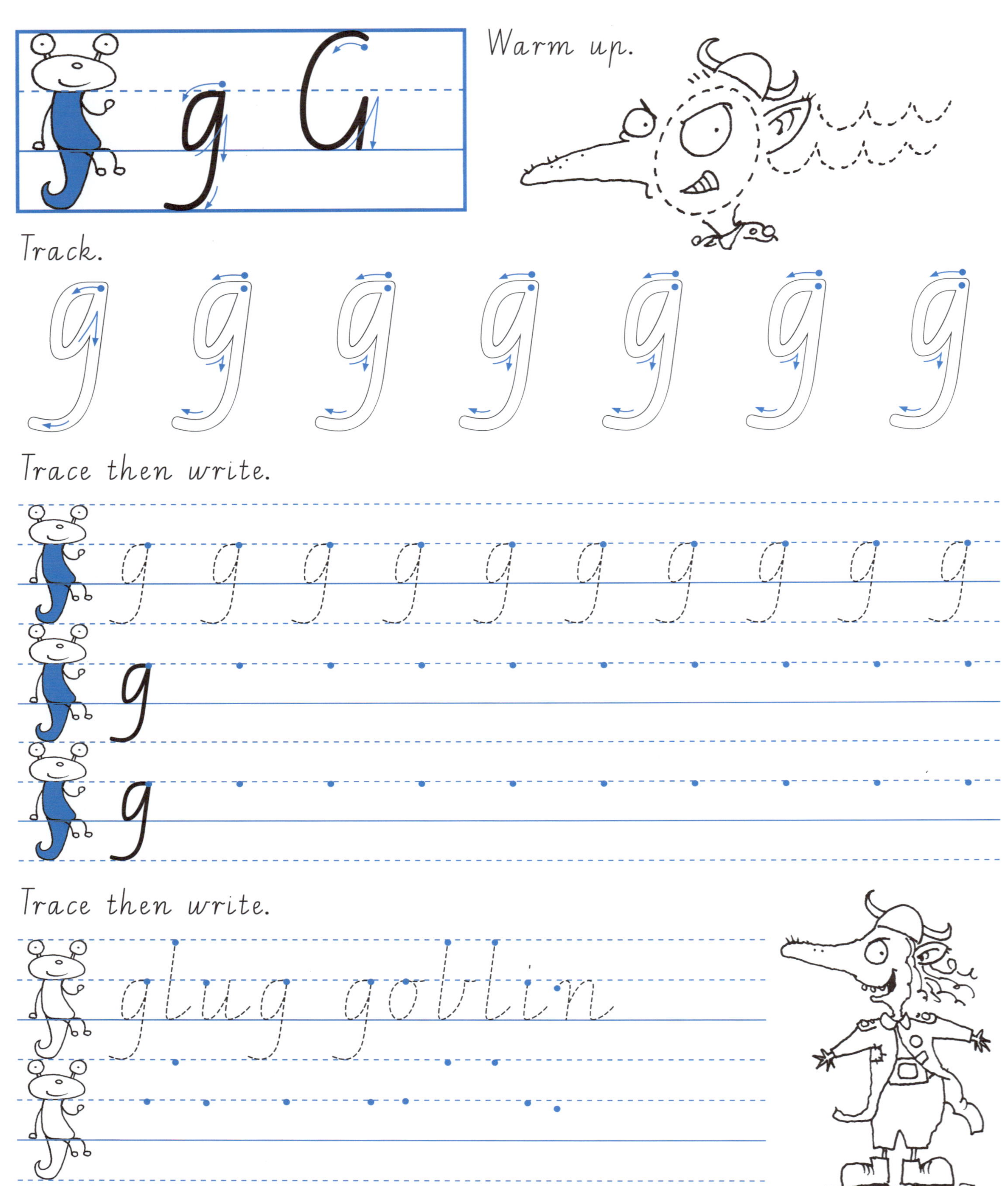

Handwriting: anticlockwise letter, body and tail letter (g).
Grammar: commands, proper nouns (Gruff, Billy).
Punctuation: direct speech, speech marks, exclamation mark.
Spelling and vocabulary: game, gasp, get, glue, go, goat, goblin, going, gone, grandma, grandpa, grape, grip.
Literary elements: alliteration, folk tale (The Three Billy Goats Gruff), story characters, onomatopoeia (glug).

Trace then write.

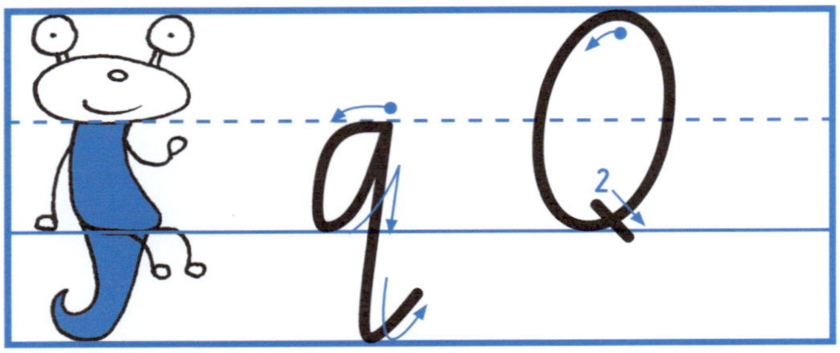

q Q

Warm up.

Track.

q q q q q q q

Trace then write.

q q q q q q q q q q

q

q

Trace then write.

quoll quit quick

Handwriting: anticlockwise letter, body and tail letter (q).
Grammar: simple sentence, proper noun (Queenie).
Punctuation: capital letter to start a sentence, full stop.
Spelling and vocabulary: equal, quail, queen, quick, quiet, quit, quite, quiz, quoll.
Literary elements: alliteration.

Trace then write.

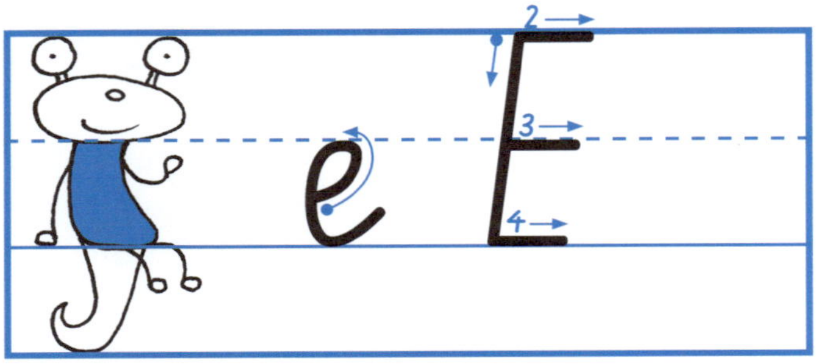

e E

Warm up.

Track.

e e e e e e e

Trace then write.

e e e e e e e e e e e

e

e

Trace then write.

elephant every eats

Handwriting: anticlockwise letter, body letter (e).
Grammar: simple sentence, saying verb (yelled), describing word/adjective (excited).
Punctuation: capital letter to start a sentence, exclamation mark, speech marks.
Spelling and vocabulary: eagle, ear, earth, eat, eating, egg, elephant, elf, even, every, extra.
Literary elements: alliteration, story character (elf), onomatopoeia (eek).

Trace then write.

Trace then write.

"Eek! Eagle!" yelled

the excited elf.

Rate your writing.

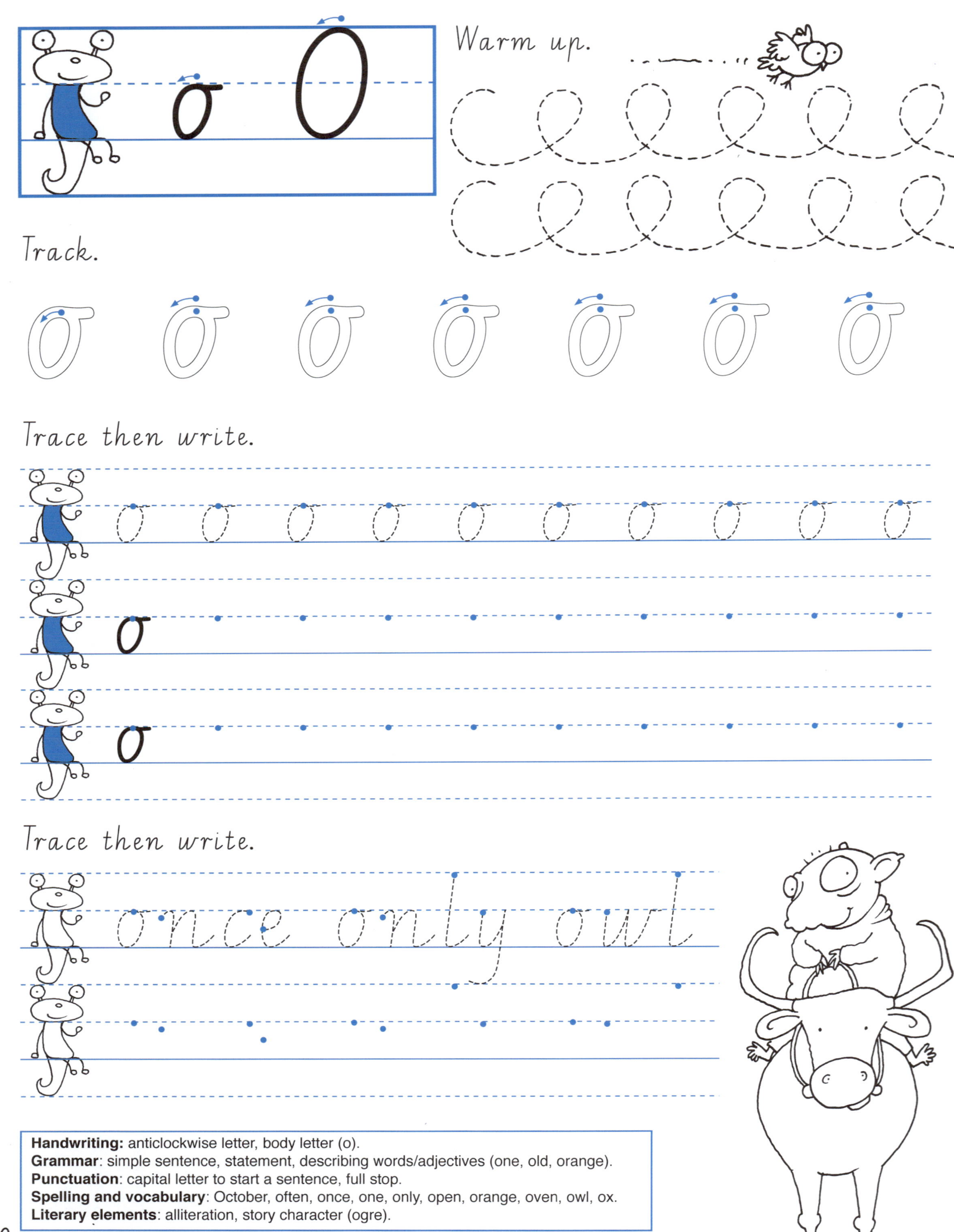

Handwriting: anticlockwise letter, body letter (o).
Grammar: simple sentence, statement, describing words/adjectives (one, old, orange).
Punctuation: capital letter to start a sentence, full stop.
Spelling and vocabulary: October, often, once, one, only, open, orange, oven, owl, ox.
Literary elements: alliteration, story character (ogre).

Trace then write.
O
o
O
Trace then write.
One old, orange ogre
is on the only ox.
Rate your writing.

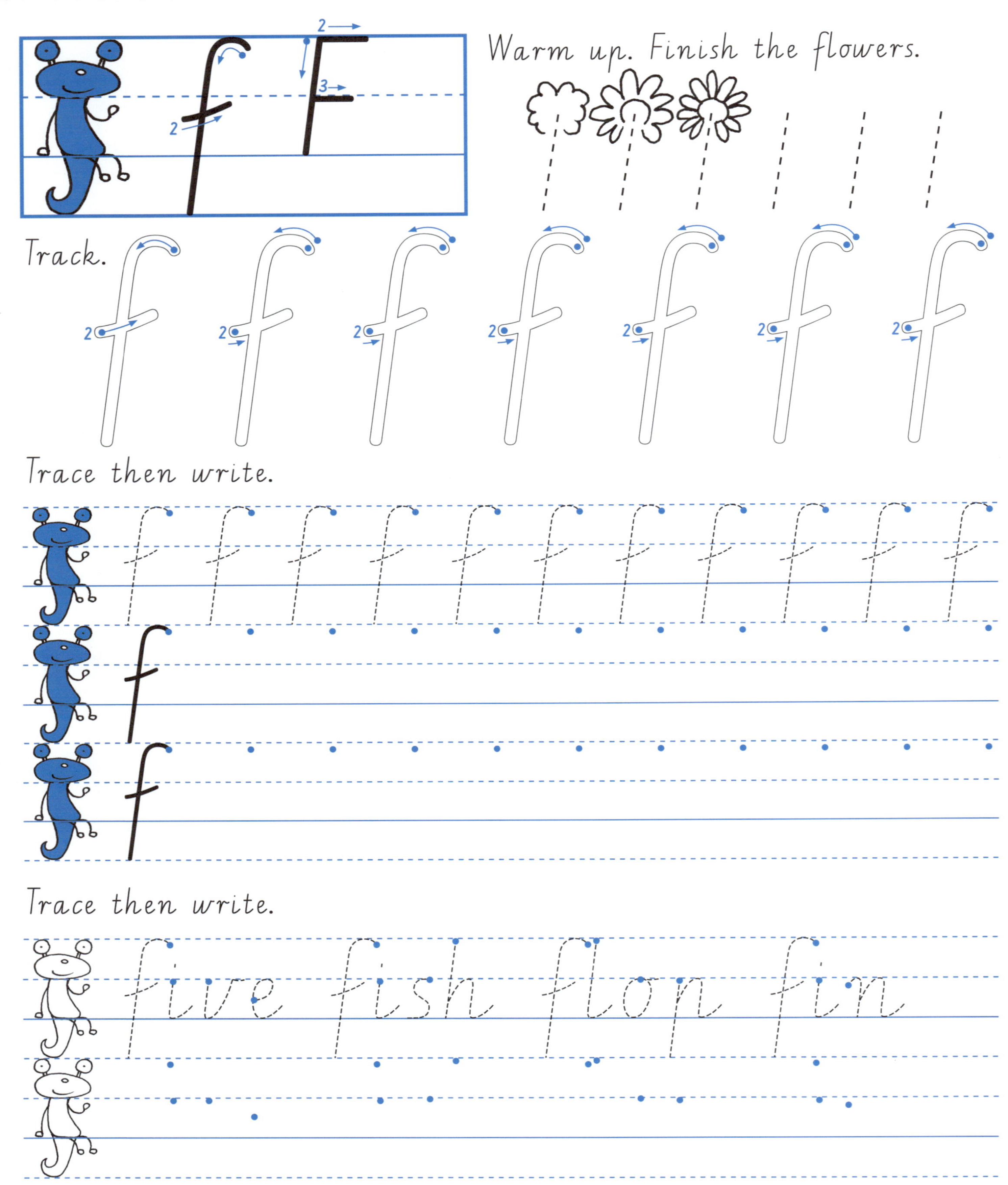

Handwriting: downstroke letter, head, body and tail letter (f).
Grammar: simple sentence, proper noun (Felix), describing word/adjective (fast), action verb (fled).
Punctuation: capital letter to start a sentence, full stop.
Spelling and vocabulary: fast, February, feel, fin, find, first, fish, fit, five, fleck, fled, flesh, flop, foam, foot, Friday, frisky, fry, frog, fun.
Literary elements: alliteration.

Trace then write.
F
f
F
Trace then write.
Fast Felix fled on
foot from the frog.
Rate your writing.

Handwriting: anticlockwise letter, body letter (s).
Grammar: simple sentence, statement, proper noun (Samson), action verb (sat), describing word/adjective (startled), saying verb (said).
Punctuation: capital letter to start a sentence, full stop.
Spelling and vocabulary: said, sand, Saturday, saw, see, send, September, seven, sister, six, slump, snail, snort, spider, squid.
Literary elements: alliteration, onomatopoeia (snort).

Trace then write.

S

s

S

Trace then write.

Samson almost sat

on a startled spider.

Rate your writing.

Handwriting: clockwise letter with rounded entry, body letter (m).
Grammar: simple sentence, action verb (munch), describing word/adjective (merry).
Punctuation: capital letter to start a sentence, full stop.
Spelling and vocabulary: mad, March, May, melon, meow, merry, mess, Monday, monkey, monster, moo, mother, mud, mum, munch.
Literary elements: alliteration.

Trace then write.

M M M

m

M

Trace then write.

Merry monkeys

munch on melons.

Rate your writing.

Handwriting: clockwise letter with rounded entry, body letter (n).
Grammar: simple sentence, how word/adverb (noisily), action verb (nibbled), proper noun (Nonna).
Punctuation: capital letter to start a sentence, full stop.
Spelling and vocabulary: name, nest, new, newt, next, nibble, nice, nine, no, noodle, not, never, Nonna, November, now.
Literary elements: alliteration.

Trace then write.

Trace then write.

Nonna noisily

nibbled noodles.

Rate your writing.

r R

Warm up.

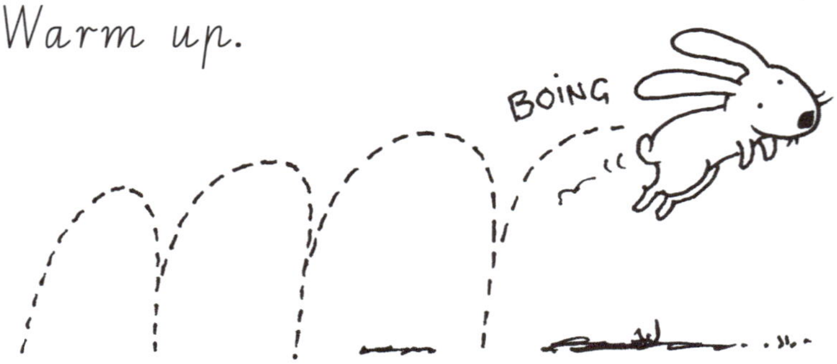

BOING

Track.

r r r r r r r

Trace then write.

r r r r r r r r r r

r

r

Trace then write.

rats reading run

Handwriting: clockwise letter with rounded entry, body letter (r).
Grammar: simple sentence, describing words/adjectives (red, rude), proper nouns (Raging Roger).
Punctuation: capital letter to start a sentence, full stop.
Spelling and vocabulary: rabbit, raft, ran, rang, rat, read, real, red, reek, reeks, ring, roast, robot, rot, rude, run, rush, rushing.
Literary elements: alliteration.

Trace then write.

Handwriting: clockwise letter with rounded entry, body letter (x).
Grammar: simple sentence, statement.
Punctuation: capital letter to start a sentence, full stop.
Spelling and vocabulary: apostrophe (don't), box, exam, fox, mix, oxen, six, T-Rex, taxi, text, wax, X-ray, xylophone.

Trace then write.

Trace then write.

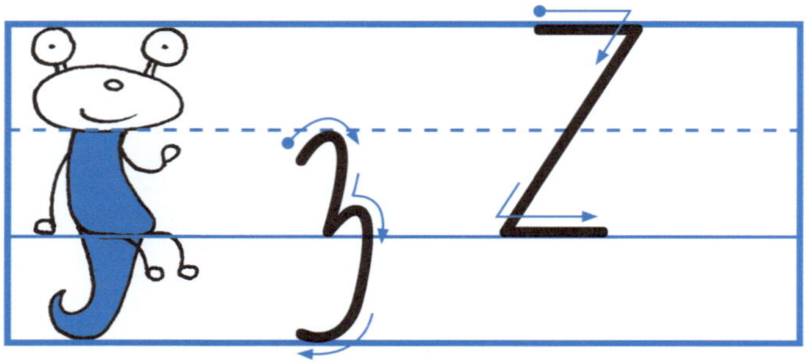

z Z

Warm up.

Track.

z z z z z z z

Trace then write.

z z z z z z z z z z z

z

z

Trace then write.

zebra whiz zoo zero

Handwriting: clockwise letter with rounded entry, body and tail letter (z).
Grammar: simple sentence/statement, proper noun (Zoe), possessive apostrophe (Zoe's).
Punctuation: capital letter to start a sentence, full stop.
Spelling and vocabulary: doze, quiz, zany, zap, zebra, zero, zest, zesty, zing, zip, zoo.
Literary elements: alliteration, onomatopoeia (whiz, zip, zap).

Trace then write.

Trace then write.

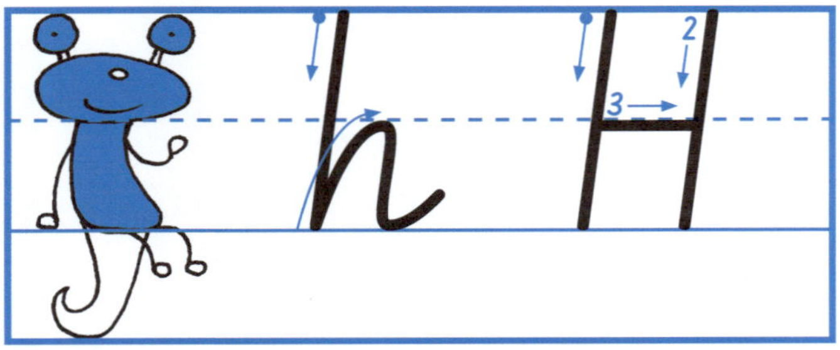

h H

Warm up.

Track.

h h h h h h

Trace then write.

h h h h h h h h h

h

h

Trace then write.

howl hiss hum help

Handwriting: clockwise letter, head and body letter (h).
Grammar: direct speech, saying verb (shouted), describing word/adjective (hungry).
Punctuation: capital letter to start a sentence, exclamation mark, speech marks.
Spelling and vocabulary: hair, hang, hawk, help, hen, hid, hide, hiss, hum, hog, home, honey, hospital, howl, hungry, heart.
Literary elements: alliteration, onomatopoeia (hiss, howl), folk tale (Hansel and Gretel).

Trace then write.

H h H

Trace then write.

"Hello!" shouted

hungry Hansel.

Rate your writing.

Handwriting: clockwise letter, head and body letter (k).
Grammar: simple sentence, proper noun (King Kong).
Punctuation: capital letter to start a sentence, full stop.
Spelling and vocabulary: key, kind, kiss, kitten, koala, silent k (knee, knew, knit, knots, know).
Literary elements: alliteration, story characters (King Kong), anthropomorphism.

Trace then write.
K K K
k
K
Clickity clack
Trace then write.
King Kong knew he
kept knitting knots.
Rate your writing.

Handwriting: clockwise letter, body and tail letter (p).
Grammar: simple sentence/statement, action verbs (poked, pushed), proper noun (Pedro).
Punctuation: capital letter to start a sentence, full stop.
Spelling and vocabulary: peep, pet, pencil, pig, pimple, pink, plop, plus, poke, pong, pony, possum, post, pumpkin, push, put, python.
Literary elements: alliteration, onomatopoeia (plop).

Trace then write.
P
p
P
Trace then write.
Pedro poked and
pushed a python.
Rate your writing.

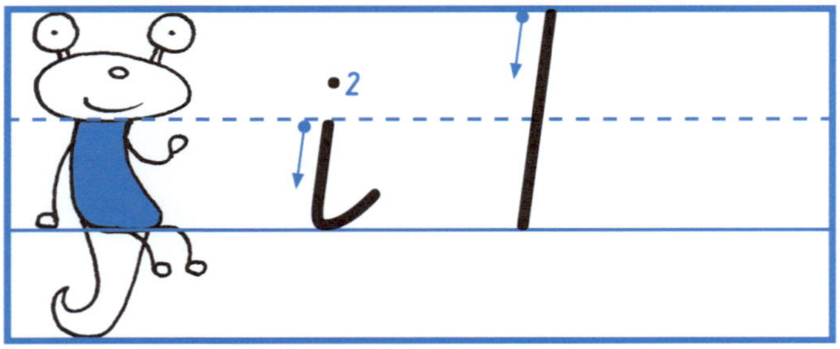

i l

Warm up.

Track.

2 i 2 i 2 i 2 i 2 i 2 i 2 i 2 i

Trace then write.

i i i i i i i i i i i i

i

i

Trace then write.

itchy iguana ink

Handwriting: i family letter, body letter (i).
Grammar: simple sentence/statement, proper noun (Iggy), describing word/adjective (itchy).
Punctuation: capital letter to start a sentence, full stop.
Spelling and vocabulary: icky, idea, idol, igloo, iguana, imp, in, ink, insect, inside, into, is, isn't, it, itchy.
Literary elements: alliteration.

Trace then write.
Scratch
scratch
Trace then write.
Iggy is in bed
ill and itchy.
Rate your writing.
ink
ink ink
ink ink ink

Handwriting: i family letter, head and body letter (t).
Grammar: simple sentence/statement, possessive (its).
Punctuation: capital letter to start a sentence, full stop.
Spelling and vocabulary: tail, tale, take, teeth, tell, Tuesday, Thursday, time, timid, took, toot, tooth, trap, try, turtle, ten, three, twelve, two.
Literary elements: alliteration, story characters (troll), onomatopoeia (toot), play on words (took its time).

Trace then write.

Trace then write.

Handwriting: i family letter, head and body letter (l).
Grammar: simple sentence/statement, proper noun (Lilly), describing words/adjectives (lovely, little), action verbs (limp, lick, leap).
Punctuation: capital letter to start a sentence, full stop.
Spelling and vocabulary: lazy, leap, left, lesson, lick, life, lift, limb, limp, lion, list, live, lizard, llama, log, lose, lost, love, lovely, lumpy.
Literary elements: alliteration.

Trace then write.

Trace then write.

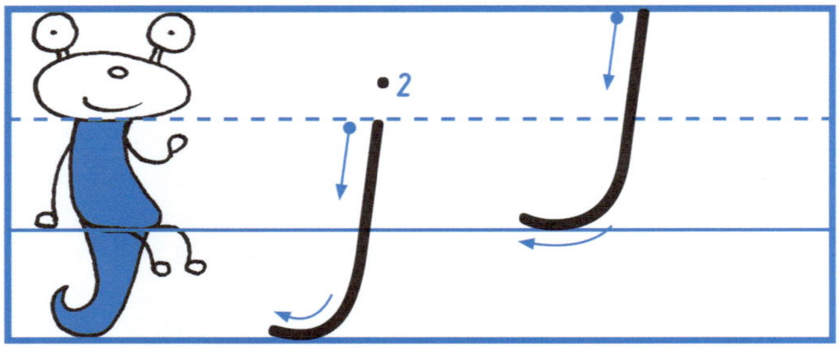

Warm up.

Track.

Trace then write.

Trace then write.

just joking jam jog

Handwriting: i family letter, body and tail letter (j).
Grammar: simple sentence/statement, action verbs (jiggles, jumps, jogs), proper noun (Jill).
Punctuation: capital letter to start a sentence, full stop.
Spelling and vocabulary: jam, jammed, January, jet, jelly bean, jiggle, joey, jog, join, joke, July, June, jump, just.
Literary elements: alliteration, nursery rhyme (Jack and Jill went up the hill).

Trace then write.

Trace then write.

Handwriting: u family letter, body letter (u).
Grammar: saying verbs (uttered), proper nouns (Uncle Uno).
Punctuation: capital letter to start a sentence, exclamation mark, speech marks.
Spelling and vocabulary: prefix un- (undo, untie, unzip), ulcer, ultra, uncle, under, until, up, upend, upon.
Literary elements: alliteration, onomatopoeia (ouch).

Trace then write.

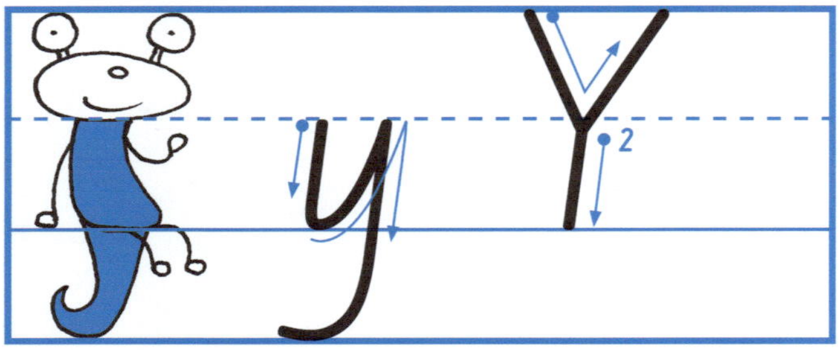

y Y

Warm up.

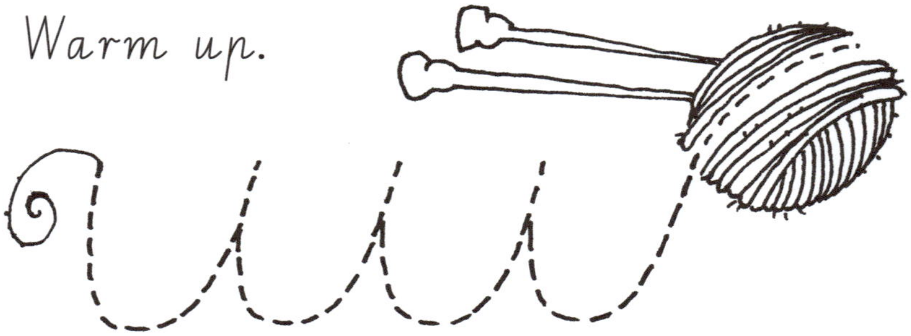

Track.

Trace then write.

y y y y y y y y y y y

y

y

Trace then write.

year yawn yes you

Handwriting: u family letter, body and tail letter (y).
Grammar: saying verb (yak).
Punctuation: capital letter to start a sentence, full stop.
Spelling and vocabulary: yacht, yak, yap, yard, yarn, yawn, year, yen, yep, yes, yeti, yoga, yolk, you, yuan, yummy.
Literary elements: alliteration, onomatopoeia (yakkity yak), anthropomorphism, speech bubble.

Trace then write.

Y Y Y

y

Y

Yakkity yak!

Trace then write.

Yaks yakkity yak

on yoga mats.

Rate your writing.

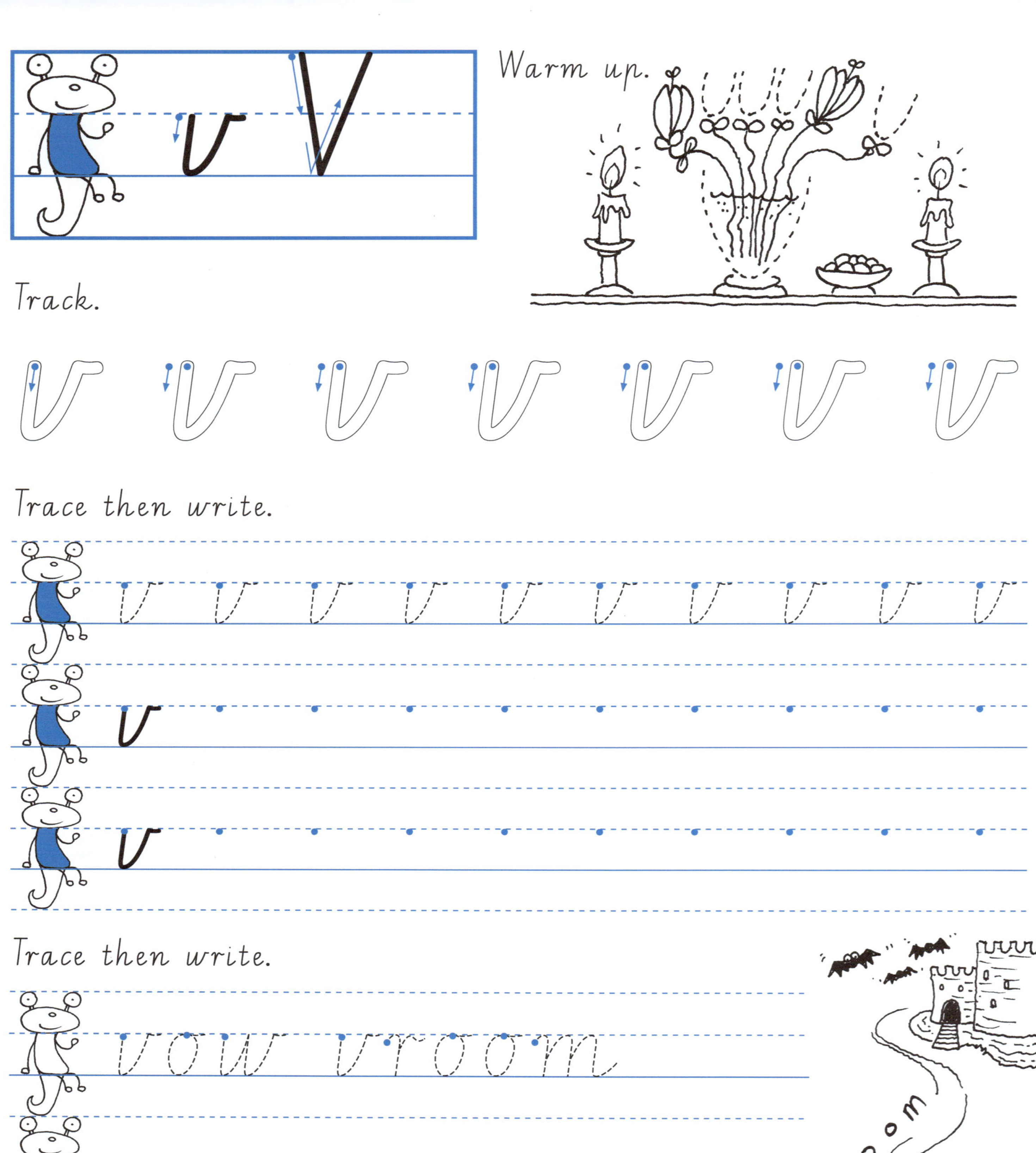

Handwriting: u family letter, body letter (v).
Grammar: simple sentence, proper nouns (Vinnie Vole).
Punctuation: capital letter to start a sentence, full stop.
Spelling and vocabulary: vain, vase, very, vest, vibe, vine, violin, volcano, vole, vote, vow.
Literary elements: alliteration, anthropomorphism, onomatopoeia (vroom).

Trace then write.

V V V

v

V

Trace then write.

Vinnie vole

was very vain.

Rate your writing.

Handwriting: u family letter, body letter (w).
Grammar: saying verb (asked), proper noun (Wally), direct speech, question.
Punctuation: capital letter to start a sentence, speech marks, question mark.
Spelling and vocabulary: wall, walrus, watermelon, was, wasp, wave, Wednesday, when, whew, which, whiz, who, wild, wilt, win, wink.
Literary elements: alliteration, anthropomorphism.

Trace then write.

W W W

w

W

Trace then write.

"Who will win?"

asked Wally.

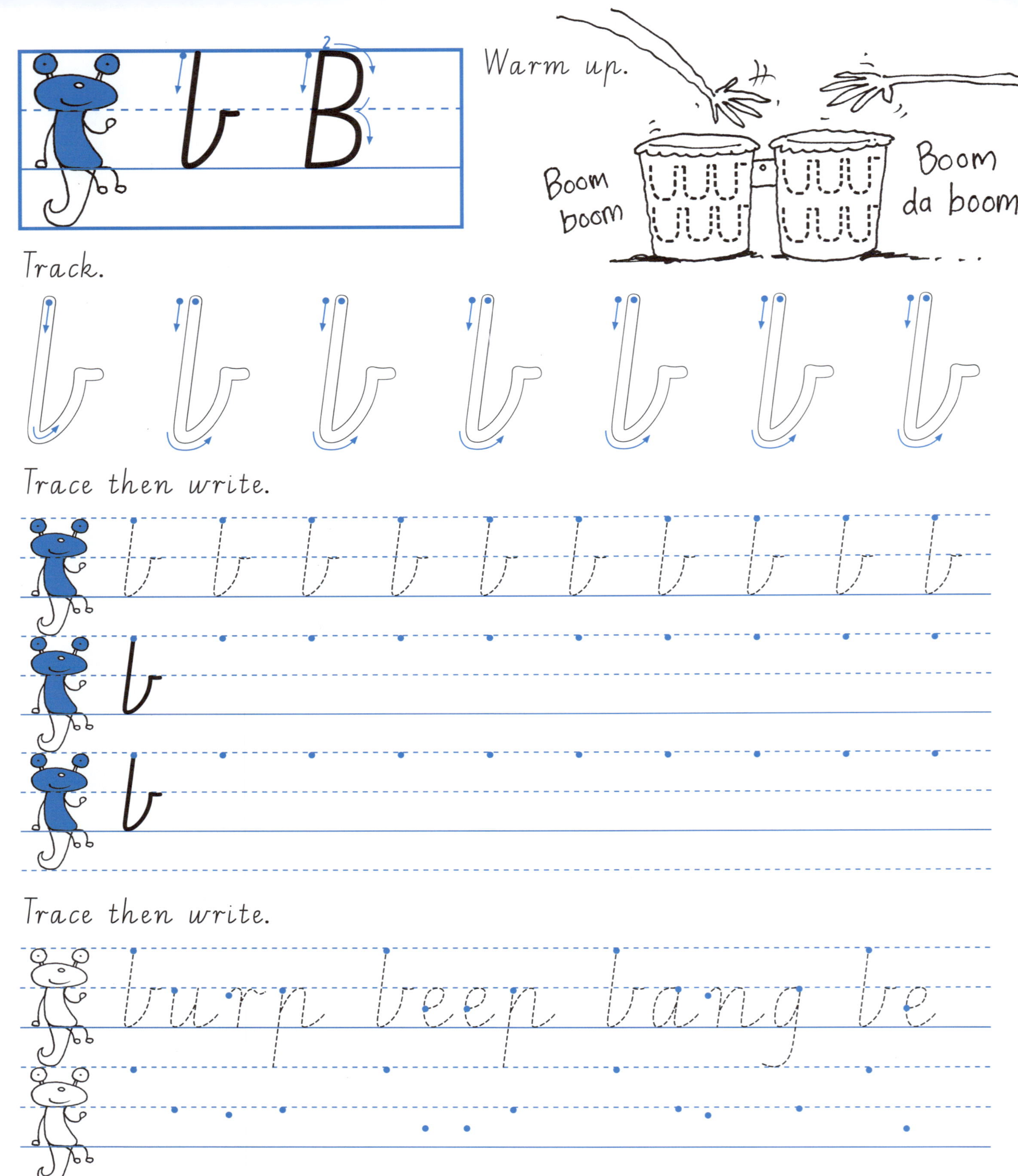

Handwriting: u family letter, head and body letter (b).
Grammar: simple sentence, action verb (boogied).
Punctuation: capital letter to start a sentence, full stop.
Spelling and vocabulary: baby, bag, banana, band, bang, bear, before, best, better, big, bird, boat, book, brag, bring, brown, burp.
Literary elements: alliteration, onomatopoeia (beep), anthropomorphism.

Trace then write.

Trace then write.

Trace then write.

Trace then write.

15 fifteen

16 sixteen

17 seventeen

18 eighteen

19 nineteen

20 twenty

30 thirty

Rate your writing.

☆ ☆☆ ☆☆☆

Trace then write.

Trace then write.

1 2

3 4

5 6

7 8

9 10

Trace.

10 20 30 40 50

60 70 80 90 100